Ye Yucky MIDDLE AGES

DON'T LET THE BARBER PULL YOUR TEETH

Could You Survive Medieval Medicine?

Carmen Bredeson
Illustrated by Gerald Kelley

Enslow Publishers, Inc.
40 Industrial Road
Box 398
Berkeley Heights, NJ 07922
USA

http://www.enslow.com

Library of Congress Cataloging-in-Publication Data

Bredeson, Carmen.
    Don't let the barber pull your teeth : could you survive medieval medicine? / by Carmen Bredeson.
        p. cm. — (Ye yucky Middle Ages)
    Summary: "Explores 'yucky' aspects of medieval medicine"—Provided by publisher.
    Includes bibliographical references and index.
    ISBN 978-0-7660-3693-2
    1. Medicine, Medieval—Juvenile literature. 2. Europe—History—476–1492—Juvenile literature.
    3. Europe—Social conditions—To 1492—Juvenile literature. I. Title.
    R141.B74 2011
    610—dc22   2010011898

Paperback ISBN 978-1-59845-373-7

Printed in China

052011 Leo Paper Group, Heshan City, Guangdong, China

10 9 8 7 6 5 4 3 2 1

To Our Readers: We have done our best to make sure all Internet Addresses in this book were active and appropriate when we went to press. However, the author and the publisher have no control over and assume no liability for the material available on those Internet sites or on other Web sites they may link to. Any comments or suggestions can be sent by e-mail to comments@enslow.com or to the address on the back cover.

Illustration Credits: © 2010 Gerald Kelley, www.geraldkelley.com

Cover Illustration: © 2010 Gerald Kelley, www.geraldkelley.com

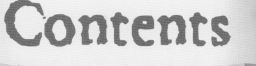

Contents

Rivers of Filth

A dozen children ran down the street, laughing and playing. They dodged pigs and jumped over chickens. As they went around a corner, one boy slipped. He fell face-first into the **gutter** at the side of the street. He came up sputtering and wiped the brown slime from his face. On he ran, after his friends.

Gutters ran along the sides of many medieval streets. They were a dumping ground for pee, poop, and animal waste. The gutter water was full of germs that cause diseases. During the Middle Ages, people did not know about germs. They did not know how diseases spread or what caused them. Filthy water did not seem dangerous to them. Dirty streets were not thought to be a threat. They were a normal part of medieval life.

> The Middle Ages were the years between 500 and 1500. This time is also called the medieval period.

Too Dirty to Drink

When it rained, dirty water flowed down the streets. It ended up in the river. Where did many medieval people get water for cooking and washing? Out of the polluted river! It is a good thing that medieval people did not drink much water. It was too dirty and full of disease-causing germs. Instead they drank wine or weak beer all day long—even the children! Most towns had wells, but the water in them was dirty too. The cleanest water around was rainwater. However, it was only as clean as the jar it was collected in.

Dirty water is a good place to catch typhoid. This disease causes high fevers, diarrhea, and headaches. When a person with typhoid goes to the bathroom, germs come out in their poop. If that poop gets into the water supply, the germs can spread. Drinking the water or washing food with it can spread typhoid. Typhoid spread easily during the Middle Ages and caused many deaths.

7

Piles of Poop Everywhere!

Medieval people went to the bathroom where they could. Sometimes it was behind a tree or a building. Most homes had small pots that people used to go to the bathroom. Each house had a cesspit outside. The cesspit was a hole in the ground that was lined with wood or stones. People dumped their waste pots into it. As the pit filled up, the smell got worse and worse. Flies feasted on the piles of poop. Then they flew into the house and landed on the food. This could pass typhoid and **dysentery** to the family.

All of the cesspits had to be cleaned out when they got full. Men were hired to do this dirty work. The men were so smelly that they had to live together in a certain area of town. Nobody else wanted to live around them. As they worked, they got covered in filthy muck.

Some houses had a garderobe or privy. This little room had a raised bench with a hole cut in the middle. Waste fell directly into a pit underneath. A few clever people built their garderobes over streams. Then the waste fell into the water and was carried away from their houses. Where did the waste end up? In the river, of course. It flowed along with the toilet paper of the day—moss, straw, or leaves.

9

Medieval streets were full of animal manure. Horses, cows, sheep, pigs, goats, and chickens roamed around the streets. They left behind smelly piles of manure. Rats and mice scurried around the piles, looking for a snack.

All of this filth seems disgusting to us today. Why did the Middle Ages have to be so dirty? The lack of clean water was one reason. Washing in dirty water doesn't do much good, so why bother? If your neighbors threw their garbage in the street, you probably would too. Medieval people did not know that diseases could be spread in water and sewage.

Medieval Misery

Not all diseases of the Middle Ages were spread by dirty water. Scurvy was a common illness during the time. We now know that it is caused by a lack of vitamin C. Most people get their vitamin C from eating fresh fruits and vegetables. But during the long medieval winters, people did not have fresh fruits and vegetables to eat. The lack of vitamin C caused bleeding gums and loose teeth. When summer came around, there were fruits and vegetables again. Some people got enough vitamin C to make their symptoms go away—until the next winter.

Smoky air caused many lung problems for medieval people. Every house had a fire pit, with a fire burning much of the time. It was used for cooking food and

heating the house. The fire made a lot of smoke. The smoke filled the air and escaped out a hole in the roof. When there was wind, the smoke blew back inside. People used candles and lanterns for light. These added to the smoky haze in the room. All of the smoke caused coughing, wheezing, and burning eyes.

Smallpox was another very serious disease. It caused a high fever, chills, and vomiting. The patient usually had a rash that turned into sores. The sores were often very large. They left deep scars on the skin, especially on the face. Smallpox could also cause blindness. The disease was easily passed from person to person. Many, many people died from smallpox.

Bathing Optional

In the Middle Ages, many people had skin rashes and sores. They didn't bathe much, so their skin got irritated. Some people bathed in rivers and streams, but it was too cold to do this during the winter.

13

Wealthy people may have taken a few baths a year. They had servants to heat water and carry the heavy buckets to a tub. That is not true in all cases, though. Most people washed their hands and faces in the morning. They also washed their hands before eating. Clothing was often made of scratchy wool. Cloth was expensive, so most people had only one set of clothes. It wasn't washed very often, if ever. Fleas and lice lived in the clothes and feasted on the bare skin.

A Feared Disease

Leprosy has long been one of the most feared skin diseases. The victim's skin and nerves are infected by germs. First the fingers and toes get numb. Then the fingers and toes might become paralyzed—or even fall off. Leprosy sometimes causes the bridge of the nose to collapse. The disease can also cause blindness. Lepers have been shunned because their disease does such horrible damage to the body.

During the Middle Ages, lepers had to wear gloves and long robes. They also had to ring bells to warn others that they

15

were near. Lepers were not allowed to enter buildings or to use the water wells in town. There were places outside the town gates for them to live.

Nobody wanted to breathe the same air as a leper. Lepers were told to stand downwind to talk. Then the air would blow the leper's breath away. People were beginning to understand that certain diseases could be passed from person to person. This was a new idea for the time.

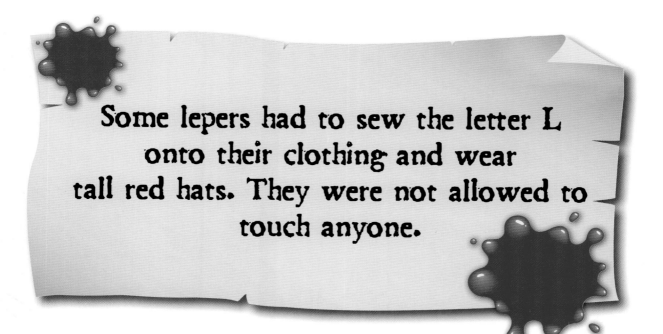

Some lepers had to sew the letter L onto their clothing and wear tall red hats. They were not allowed to touch anyone.

What's Up, Doc?

Doctors in the Middle Ages didn't really know what caused illness. They went to medical schools. They read about diseases in books. But few of them knew what a human body looked like inside. Most religions would not allow medical students to cut open and study the bodies of dead people. So students cut up pigs and other animals. They studied the animals' organs. Were human organs the same? After 1300, the practice of dissecting human bodies became more common. Medical students could finally see what humans looked like inside.

A Sip of Urine, Anyone?

Medieval doctors were taught that the body was made up of four **humors**: blood, yellow bile, black bile, and phlegm. It was believed that people got sick if the humors were out of balance. In order to cure a sick person, the humors had to be balanced again. Who balanced the humors and how did they do it?

Rich people called for a doctor when they got sick. Doctors usually did not treat poor people. First the doctor looked at his patient's skin color. Then he might take his pulse. Next he asked the patient to urinate in a glass jar. The doctor held the jar up to the light to see the color. This was called "reading" the urine. Some doctors had a color wheel. It showed the different shades of urine and what each one meant. The colors ranged from clear to yellow to red to black. Obviously, red or black urine was not a good sign. The best color for urine was bright gold. After looking at the color, the doctor smelled the urine. Then he TASTED it! Did it taste sweet or bitter? Examining the urine helped the doctor decide if a patient's humors were out of balance.

18

Barbers at Work

The main way to get the humors back in balance was to bleed
the patient. Doctors did not do this messy work themselves.
They called in a barber surgeon. Barber surgeons did not go to
medical schools. In fact, most of them could not read or write.
They were barbers, who cut hair and shaved faces. But they
also set bones, pulled teeth, bled people, sewed up cuts, and

did other kinds of surgery. Why would a barber do this kind of work? Because he had sharp scissors and knives.

The red and white barber poles we still see today date from this time. Some barber surgeons advertised their work by wrapping bloody rags around a pole. Others left a bowl of blood in the window. Many barber surgeons traveled from town to town. They set up tents at county fairs. People lined up to have teeth pulled and wounds stitched up.

How did the barbers know what to do? Books from the medieval period had charts in them. They showed which veins to cut to heal each part of the body. People believed that too much blood in one part of the body led to an imbalance. By taking blood from the sick part, balance would be restored. Many thought that blood was made in the liver and then

There was a belief in the Middle Ages that little worms in the teeth caused tooth decay.

flowed out to the rest of the body. Nobody knew that blood flowed back to the heart and was pumped around the body.

Doctors thought that the blood in an arm stayed in the arm. Blood in the foot stayed in the foot. The surgeon cut a vein to take blood from the sick part of the body. He watched as blood dripped into a bowl. When there was enough, he put pressure on the vein to stop the bleeding. A person who was bled too often could die from lack of blood. If an artery was accidentally cut by the surgeon, the patient could bleed so much that he would die.

Let Us Suck Your Blood

Leeches were also used to bleed people. When a leech bites a person it releases a substance into their blood. This keeps the blood from clotting. When blood clots, it gets thick and stops flowing. Blood needs to stay thin for a leech to suck it. When the leech is full, it drops off of the skin. Sometimes a surgeon wanted to take out a lot of blood. Then several leeches were used at one time.

Tools of the Trade

Barber surgeons had knives to slice the skin and saws to cut through bones. They also had needles and thread to sew up wounds. Metal pokers that looked like branding irons were used on some wounds. They were heated in a fire and put directly on the wound. The burning heat stopped blood from flowing. It sealed the cut. Surgeons also had special tools for pulling arrowheads out of flesh. Wars were going on all the time. There were plenty of men who had been wounded in battle.

Leeches are very good at sucking blood. A few big ones can drain all of the blood from a rabbit. Leeches are still used today. Sometimes a person's finger or toe gets cut off. Then a surgeon tries to sew it back on. It is hard to get the blood flowing again in the little veins. The blood backs up and cuts off the circulation. Then the finger or toe dies. Leeches are sometimes used to suck out the pools of blood. They also help thin the blood and keep it moving.

Risky Business

Any kind of surgery during the Middle Ages was very risky. Most patients were awake for their operations. It took several men to hold down a screaming patient. Patients often died of shock because of the pain. Sometimes the patient was knocked out, but that was very dangerous, too. Dwale was a drink used to put people to sleep before surgery. It was made out of vinegar, pig's bile, and some wild plants. The patient drank the mixture until he fell asleep, maybe forever.

People who survived surgery often ended up with massive infections. None of the surgical instruments were cleaned between operations. Doctors did not know to wash their hands. However, medieval people did pour alcohol on wounds. They did not understand that alcohol kills germs, but knew it helped with healing.

A Hole in the Head

Trepanning was one kind of operation that was done during the Middle Ages. A hole or holes were drilled in the skull of a person suffering from headaches. The drill had a wooden handle with a sharp metal point on the end. A strap on the handle was pulled back and forth to turn the drill. The holes were supposed to help the pain escape. Holes were also drilled into the skulls of people suffering from mental illness. People thought the holes allowed evil spirits to leave the head. If a person survived the operation, new bone eventually grew over the holes.

No Blinking!

Another surgery involved the eyes. A condition called a cataract makes the lens of the eye get cloudy. Eventually the lens is so cloudy that everything the person sees looks blurry. Medieval surgeons tried to fix the problem. They poked a sharp knife or needle into the **cornea** of the eye. Then the cloudy

Broken bones were set using wooden splints. If the break was too bad, the leg or arm was usually cut off, or amputated.

lens was pushed to the bottom of the eye. If the surgery went well, the patient could see a little better. Sometimes the lens burst and all vision was lost. Sometimes the surgery caused an infection that killed the patient.

Medieval Cures

During the Middle Ages, people used herbs, flowers, seeds, and minerals to treat illnesses. People in big towns could buy medicine from an **apothecary**. Apothecaries were like the pharmacists of today. They treated the sick and prescribed various remedies.

Apothecaries had gardens where they grew many of the herbs they used in medicine. Their shops were filled with jars of ingredients. The apothecary used a recipe for each medicine. He picked out the right ingredients for the remedy. Then he put them into a bowl called a mortar. He ground the mixture together with a stick called a pestle.

Sometimes the apothecary cooked herbs and spices in a big pot. He poured the syrup he made into

bottles and sold it as a cure for different illnesses. Some of the remedies worked and still work today. Others were useless, but many people tried them anyway, hoping to get well.

Weird Remedies

Tying a piece of crosswort to the head was one cure for headaches. People believed the herb had to be tied on with a red bandanna for the cure to work. Fried black snails were put on spider bites to cure them. Poop from a goose was used to heal cuts. The heads of fried dung beetles and crickets were eaten to get rid of stones in the bladder. How did some people stop nosebleeds? By putting pig poop on their noses!

30

These remedies seem silly to us now. But people during the Middle Ages did not have the medicine we have today. They were willing to try anything to cure their health problems.

Remedies That Worked!

Bark from willow trees helped ease pain and reduce fever. People boiled willow bark and leaves into a syrup. They also chewed the bark for toothaches. Ginger and mint plants were prescribed for stomach problems. Mint teas and ginger are still popular treatments for upset stomachs. Some people took the herb feverfew for headaches. Some people still do today! Doctors in the Middle Ages used parts of the poppy plant to treat pain. Some of today's strongest painkillers come from the poppy plant.

Wise Women

People in small towns and villages did not usually have access to doctors or even to barber surgeons. Village women knew about herbal remedies and treated their families and friends. They planted herb gardens with the things that had seemed to work in the past. Also, there were women in many villages

31

32

who were known as healers or wise women. Most of the wise women could not read or write. They learned from experience. They passed their knowledge to the next generation, just as their mothers had taught them.

The Dangerous Business of Being Born

Midwives are women who deliver babies. That was something men did not do in the Middle Ages. Childbirth was a very dangerous time in a medieval woman's life. Many women died. Many medieval women gave birth a dozen times. Girls were allowed to marry at age twelve. They had many years ahead to have babies.

Infections were a big problem for both mothers and babies. As many as half of the children born during the Middle Ages died by age five. Childhood illness and infection caused most of the deaths. Accidents and burns also took the lives of many children. Every home had an open fireplace. Babies and small children sometimes got too close to the fire.

Babies who survived birth were wrapped in long strips of linen with only their faces showing. This was done to keep the baby warm. It also kept their arms and legs straight. People thought the baby's arms and legs would grow crooked if they were not wrapped tightly during infancy.

A Gallon of Ale a Day!

Monks ran the first hospitals. They gave aid to the sick and the poor. The place where monks live is called a **monastery**. Monasteries were usually located out in the country. Many patients got better simply because the monasteries were away from crowded towns. A lot of monks believed in cleanliness.

The average life expectancy during the Middle Ages was about 40 years old.

They bathed their patients and washed their clothes and bed linens. This helped cut down on infections.

The monks also gave healthy food to sick people to make them stronger. And each patient got a gallon of ale to drink every day! The monks did not bleed their patients. This was the best treatment of all. Taking blood from sick people only made them weaker. It did nothing to help cure diseases.

36

CHAPTER 6

Death to Millions

The plague that was later to be called the Black Death entered Italy in 1346. It came on several ships from Asia. Aboard these ships were sailors who were dead or dying. As soon as the ships docked, hundreds of black rats crawled down the ropes and scurried ashore.

The rats were crawling with fleas that carried plague germs. The fleas infected the local rats and then moved on to the people.

When an infected flea bit someone, the plague germ entered the person's blood.

But nobody knew at the time that fleas and their rat hosts caused this terrible disease. Ships carrying plague entered other ports. Soon the disease spread to many countries.

The first symptoms of the plague were fever, coughing, and vomiting blood. Then very painful swellings called **buboes** formed. They caused hard lumps in some glands, such as those in armpits or behind the ears. The buboes were red at first. Then they turned black and got infected. The infection spread to the bloodstream. This killed many people within a week or two. This kind of plague was later called the bubonic plague.

Another form, called **pneumonic** plague, also developed. In some ways, this form was even more deadly. When the plague bacteria got into the lungs, it destroyed lung tissue. Its victims did not get enough oxygen. They coughed and wheezed, trying to breathe. The coughing spread tiny droplets of bacteria into the air. The droplets could infect anyone nearby.

It took fleas to spread the bubonic plague. But sick people spread pneumonic plague to those around them.

It was common for whole families to die of this kind of plague when they passed it to one another.

Doctors told people to leave town and go into the country. Get away from the sick! Some of the people leaving were getting the plague themselves. They spread their germs to other towns. They also carried infected fleas to nearby villages.

Doctors bled plague victims and only made them weaker. They also cut open the buboes to try and let out the "poison." Then they sealed the wounds with hot pokers. If that did not kill the patient, the plague germs did. The plague killed quickly. People were known to go to bed healthy and die the next day. More than one third of the population of Europe died

Doctors tried to protect themselves when they treated plague victims. Some wore long leather gowns, gloves, and masks filled with herbs.

during the 1346–1350 **epidemic**. That was probably about 25 million people—the actual number may have been higher.

Too Many Bodies

So many people died of the plague that their bodies could not be buried fast enough. Cemeteries ran out of space. Whole families died. Villages were wiped out. Bodies were dragged out of houses and left in the street. Huge pits were dug and bodies were dumped into the pits. Soon there were too many to haul away, and the bodies piled up. Wild dogs and pigs feasted on the corpses!

A New Society

The plague changed society. So many people died that there were not enough peasant workers. Crops rotted in the fields. Those who survived asked for higher wages. Rich landowners needed the peasants. Without workers in their fields, the landowners could not make any money. Before the plague, peasants were little more than slaves. After the plague, they were able to demand better working conditions and higher wages.

The plague returned many times. But it was never again as deadly as the epidemic of 1346–1350. It only appears occasionally today. In the United States, ten to fifteen people get the plague each year. It is usually treated with antibiotics.

Medicine Then and Now

Medical treatment during the Middle Ages seems simple and crude to us today. We have modern hospitals and pharmacies full of medications. Doctors can treat everything from athlete's foot to heart disease. But what will people in one thousand years say about our medicine? Many of our treatments will probably look simple and crude to them. We need to remember that each generation does the best it can with the knowledge it has. Each generation builds on what the previous one has learned.

Doctors and barber surgeons in the Middle Ages began to operate and to learn about the human body. Their work helped make our medicine what it is today. Hopefully the things our doctors and scientists are learning now will help make the lives of future generations even better.

43

Words to Know

apothecary (uh PAH thuh ka ree)—A person who made and sold medicine.

buboes (BOO bohs)—Painful swellings on the body of a person infected with the plague.

cornea (KOR nee uh)—The clear film that covers the colored part of the eye.

dysentery (DIS in teh ree)—A disease that causes diarrhea.

Words to Know

epidemic (eh pih DEH mik)—A disease that makes a large number of people sick at the same time.

gutter (GUH tur)—A ditch along the side of a road.

humors (HYOO murs)—The four fluids of the body in medieval medicine.

monastery (MON uh stair ee)—A religious house where monks live.

pneumonic (noo MAH nik)—Something that affects the lungs.

Further Reading

BOOKS

Lynette, Rachel. **Bubonic Plague.** Farmington Hills, Mich.: KidHaven Press, 2004.

Padrino, Mercedes. **Cities and Towns in the Middle Ages.** Milwaukee: World Almanac Library, 2006.

Rodriguez, Ana Maria. **Edward Jenner: Conqueror of Smallpox.** Berkley Heights, N.J.: Enslow Publishers, Inc., 2006.

Senker, Cath. **The Black Death, 1347–1350: The Plague Spreads Across Europe.** Chicago: Raintree, 2006.

Woods, Michael. **The History of Medicine.** Minneapolis: Twenty-First Century Books, 2006.

Internet Addresses

The Black Death
**http://medievaleurope.mrdonn.org/
plague.html**

Medieval Medicine
http://www.intermaggie.com/med/index.php

The Middle Ages—Health
**http://www.learner.org/interactives/
middleages/health.html**

Index